Dorset

Compiled by
Dennis and Jan Kelsall

Acknowledgements

My thanks for the valuable advice and numerous useful leaflets that I obtained from the local authorities and the various tourist information centres throughout the area.

Text:	Dennis and Jan Kelsall
	Revised text:
	2006, Sue Viccars
	2008, David Hancock
Photography:	Dennis and Jan Kelsall
Editorial:	Ark Creative (UK) Ltd
Design:	Ark Creative (UK) Ltd

© Crimson Publishing, a division of Crimson Business Ltd

ISBN: 978-0-7117-5005-0

While every care has been taken to ensure the accuracy of the route directions, the publishers cannot accept responsibility for errors or omissions, or for changes in details given. The countryside is not static: hedges and fences can be removed, field boundaries can be altered, footpaths can be rerouted and changes in ownership can result in the closure or diversion of some concessionary paths. Also, paths that are easy and pleasant for walking in fine conditions may become slippery, muddy and difficult in wet weather, while stepping stones across rivers and streams may become impassable.

If you find an inaccuracy in either the text or maps, please write to Crimson Publishing at the address below.

First published 2003
by Jarrold Publishing
Revised and reprinted 2006, 2008.

This edition first published in Great Britain 2008 by Crimson Publishing, a division of:
Crimson Business Ltd
Westminster House, Kew Road
Richmond, Surrey, TW9 2ND
www.totalwalking.co.uk

Printed in Singapore. 4/08

Front cover: Old Harry Rocks
Previous page: Athelhampton House

Contents

Keymap

SCALE 1:384 615 or 1 INCH to about 6 MILES 1CM to 3.8KM

0   2   4   6   8   10 KILOMETRES   15

0   2   4   6   MILES 8   10

KEYMAP HEIGHTS SHOWN IN METRES

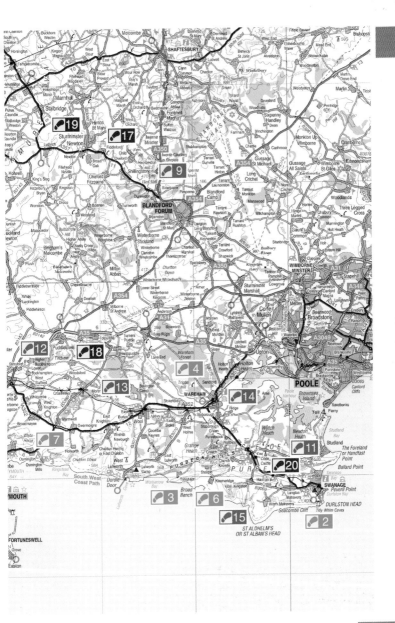

Introduction

Situated about halfway along the southern fringe of Britain, Dorset is arguably England at its most charming, a gentle, rolling landscape peppered with picturesque villages whose very names hark back to some bygone age and provoke more than usual curiosity. It is a place relatively unspoilt by the modern world, with few large towns, no motorways and the greater part of its area still devoted to the activity that has sustained it for centuries, the working of the land. Within its small compass, there is as much variety as anywhere in the country and, because it is compact, the county is easily explored on foot, by far the best way to enjoy its many qualities.

Dorset's chalk uplands and rolling limestone hills barely top 900 ft (274m) above sea level, but offer some of the finest views in the south of England. Grazed for centuries, the summer grasslands are ablaze with a mass of wildflowers that would rival many an alpine meadow, the shimmering surface alive with the dancing of countless butterflies in their flitting search for nectar. To the east, surrounding the tide-washed marshes that fringe Poole Harbour, are remnants of a once vast sandy heath. In the past, it supported poor grazing and scrubby woodland but, during the late 19th and early 20th centuries, many areas were improved

Worth Matravers village pond

as farmland, afforested with commercial timber or exploited for housing. Yet much remains in its 'natural' state and is today valued for the wildlife it supports, in particular, all six of Britain's reptiles have a home there, including the rare slow worm and sand lizard. With the adoption of more sympathetic planting and management programmes, even the forest areas are now developing as important habitats and, of course, offer many opportunities for human recreation. In the valleys, lazy rivers wind through a patchwork of lush water meadows, where herds of grazing dairy cattle complete a timeless picture. The entire coast is captivating, and ranges from spectacular and wild cliff-top scenery to attractive traditional family seaside resorts. With such rich loveliness in a countryside that supports so many important wildlife habitats, it is little wonder that almost 45 per cent of the county is included within an AONB, (Area of Outstanding Natural Beauty). That same recognition extends to the coastline, most of which is classified as Heritage Coast.

Many of the walks in this collection explore this wealth and diversity of Dorset's natural resources, such as Golden Cap, the highest point along the whole southern coast, and the Purbeck Downs, from which there are superlative views. Not to be missed either are nature reserves like that on Durlston Head, where, not only can you enjoy an amazing abundance of flowers, butterflies and birds, but with luck, watch dolphins, or even pilot whales, playing off the coast. Sadly, at the time of writing, the coast path between Stonebarrow and Lyme Regis has been re-routed along inland roads and tracks because of major landslip, and popularity and commercialism lessens the enjoyment of another favourite spot, the stretch between Lulworth Cove and Durdle Door. Yet, Lulworth is still worth seeing, and is perhaps best visited in the relative quiet of the evening, when a setting sun often enhances the view. Another gem to explore on your own is Brownsea Island, a wonderful heath and woodland nature reserve where the first camp of the Scout movement was held in 1907.

Dorset has a wealth of historical sites and associations, not least of which are the many hill forts and prehistoric burial sites scattered across the downs. The walk onto the most famous one, Maiden Castle outside Dorchester, needs no description. Instead, others equally as impressive have been included here. The fort on Hod Hill, for example, actually

Playing on the beach at Seatown

covers a larger area than Maiden Castle and also contains a Roman fort, while its neighbour on Hambledon Hill is quite spectacular and shares its site with much older Neolithic earthworks. From a later age, the castle at Corfe is one of the country's most dramatic ruins and the walk incorporates the excitement of a steam train journey as well as passing burial sites from the Neolithic and Bronze Ages. Another ramble features one of Dorset's enigmas, the Cerne Abbas Giant, a distinctive chalk figure of whose origins no one is really sure. More readily recognisable is Dorset's other example of hill art outside Osmington, the proud mounted figure of George III.

Several of Dorset's interesting buildings are featured too, such as the magnificent 15th-century Athelhampton House, Fiddleford Manor with its exquisite timbered roof, Norman churches at Studland and St Aldhelm's Head and a lovely survivor from the Saxon era, St Martin's at Wareham, built above the town walls, which are more than a century older. Other walks visit places linked with some of the county's famous people. You do not have to travel far in Dorset before coming across a village, house or pub that was thinly disguised in the novels of Thomas Hardy. His stories were woven around the life, customs and superstitions of a world already disappearing as he grew up in the mid-19th century, yet little imagination is needed to bring it all back to life. The other Hardy, Sir Thomas Masterman, is equally famous, having supported his dying Admiral, Horatio Nelson, after the Battle of Trafalgar, though fewer people perhaps know that he, too, came from a tiny Dorset village, Portesham. The memory of 'Lawrence of Arabia' also draws many visitors to this part of the world, and there is a walk linking the places associated with him. Steeped in the history of the trade union movement is the unassuming village of Tolpuddle, where a fine museum vividly portrays the story of the martyrs, who are still remembered in an annual church service and colourful rally.

Short or long, none of these walks will present any great difficulty and any steep ups and downs are soon accomplished. Everywhere, there is something of interest to distract the attention and more often than not you will find a bird, flower or insect that you have not come across before. So, take along a pocket guide to help identify the wildlife and, if you have them, a pair of small binoculars will prove more than useful.

With the introduction of 'gps enabled' walks, you will see that this book now includes a list of waypoints alongside the description of the walk. We have included these so that you can enjoy the full benefits of gps should you wish to. Gps is an amazingly useful and entertaining navigational aid, and you do not need to be computer literate to enjoy it.

GPS waypoint co-ordinates add value to your walk. You will now have the extra advantage of introducing 'direction' into your walking which will enhance your leisure walking and make it safer. Use of a gps brings greater confidence and security and you will find you cover ground a lot faster should you need to.

For essential information on map reading and basic navigation, read the *Pathfinder Guide Map Reading Skills* by outdoor writer, Terry Marsh (ISBN 978-0-7117-4978-8). For more information on using your gps, read the *Pathfinder Guide GPS for Walkers*, by gps teacher and navigation trainer, Clive Thomas (ISBN 978-0-7117-4445-5). Both titles are available in bookshops or can be ordered online at www.totalwalking.co.uk

1 *Lambert's Castle*

START Car park beside B3165, 4½ miles (7.2km) east of Axminster

DISTANCE 2 miles (3.2km)

TIME 1¼ hours

PARKING Car park

ROUTE FEATURES Woodland and field tracks; moderate climb at end; paths may be muddy after rain

Many of Dorset's hilltops still bear signs of settlement by native British tribes; earthen banks and ditches raised to protect the scattered communities who farmed the open rolling downs. Although trees again cloak the slopes of Lambert's Castle Hill, the fort remains an impressive sight, and the surrounding woodland provides an opportunity for a delightful ramble.

From a five-bar gate at the top of the car park by an information panel, follow a gently rising path onto the open heath, keeping parallel to the edge of a wood lying to the left. Shortly passing through a gap in a grassy bank, the way continues ahead through the centre of the ancient enclosure.

Ⓐ Leave at the far-left corner of the earthwork into woodland to a gate, where a clear track swings left down through the trees. When it eventually ends at a tarmac lane, turn left to a road junction.

Although you might not be lucky enough to see a roe deer, can you recognise their footprints?

Path onto Lambert's Castle Hill

PUBLIC TRANSPORT None

REFRESHMENTS Bottle Inn at nearby Marshwood (1¼ miles/2km)

PUBLIC TOILETS None

ORDNANCE SURVEY MAP Explorer 116 (Lyme Regis & Bridport)

Bracken-clad earthworks of Lambert's Castle

At almost 840 ft (256m) above sea level **Lambert's Castle Hill** offers a fine outlook over the surrounding countryside, despite the woodland that now encroaches upon its summit. The strategic importance recognised by the Iron Age settlers, who threw up the earthwork defences around their settlement, was again exploited at the beginning of the 19th century, when England was threatened with invasion by Napoleon. With a clear line of sight across the surrounding countryside, the hilltop was one of a chain of vantage points on which semaphores were built, whereby messages could be rapidly transmitted between the Government in London and the main naval base at Plymouth.

B Take care crossing to another track opposite, Hawkmoor Hill, which leads downwards between the trees. After some 250 yds (229m), look for a waymarked field track, leaving through a gate on the left. Beyond the field it continues through woodland, later narrowing to a path. Farther on, through a small gate on the left, the way diverts briefly along a fenced path at the field edge, avoiding a stream gully. Return to the track beyond, which carries on, shortly passing a barn before ending through a gate at a concrete crossing track.

The **woodlands and heath** surrounding Lambert's Castle are particularly luxuriant, supporting a wide range of plants such as tormentil, catsear and cow-wheat. From early spring, a succession of flowers brings colour to the clearings and margins, while the darker corners are rich in ferns and lichens. Although often hidden in the foliage, songbirds betray their presence with characteristic calls, and roe deer tread quietly through the shadows.

ⓒ Walk left as far as a white marker-post at a bend, there branching off left through a gate into the bottom of a field. Climb steeply away on a diagonal line to find a stile in the top boundary, beyond which a stepped path leads out to the road. Cross to a path

opposite that rises to the right through trees and bracken to a track. The car park then lies just a short walk to the left. ●

The woodland below Lambert's Castle Hill

GPS WAYPOINTS

| 🖊 SY 366 988 | Ⓑ SY 373 993 |
| Ⓐ SY 371 991 | Ⓒ SY 364 991 |

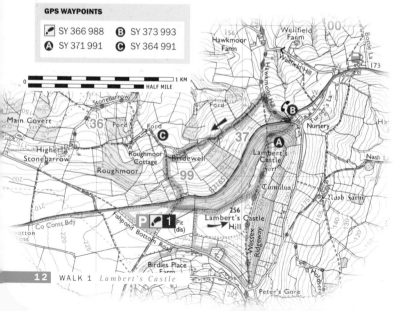

Durlston Head

START Durlston Country Park

DISTANCE 2 miles (3.2km)

TIME 1¼ hours

PARKING Car park (Pay and Display)

ROUTE FEATURES Downland grass paths; moderate climbs; paths may be slippery when wet

Once heavily quarried for its high quality Purbeck limestone, the headland and adjacent cliffs now form part of a splendid nature reserve. This short ramble winding through the numerous paths that criss-cross the downs reveals some of its many secrets.

Wander down from the south east corner of the car park (the side farthest from the visitor centre), on a drive signed to Durlston Castle. Carry on beside the café, and where the way subsequently divides, bear left to The Globe.

A Steps continue to the Coast Path at the bottom, which you should then follow around to the right, soon passing the entrance to Tilly Whim Caves. Beyond, the cliff path passes above former quarry workings before dipping to cross a gully and then climbing below the lighthouse on Anvil Point.

Durlston Castle

PUBLIC TRANSPORT Bus service to Durlston Country Park

REFRESHMENTS The Lookout Café and picnic tables near car park

PUBLIC TOILETS By visitor centre

ORDNANCE SURVEY MAP Explorer OL15 (Purbeck & South Dorset)

B Walk up to the lighthouse entrance and there leave the Coast Path, following a service drive away from the cliffs along the valley you have just crossed. Shortly, just before reaching an open gateway, climb to a kissing-gate above to the left, and continue upwards, aiming left of the high point. Soon levelling, the way continues through another gate along the crest shortly bringing you to yet another lateral wall.

C Just beyond the wall, go right on a path skirting scrub to find a gate back through the wall, 100 yds (91m) to the north. Through that, a gently meandering and undulating path returns across the top of Round Down. After crossing a couple of walls, the way eventually joins the tarmac track rising from the lighthouse. Follow it ahead through a final wall and then turn left on a path signed back to the Visitor Centre. ●

In early summer, the **chalk grasslands** above the cliffs are ablaze with the colour of countless flowers, and some 400 different species have been recorded. It is one of the few places in England where you can find the early spider orchid, as well as the more common pyramidal and spotted varieties. Among the many butterflies attracted to the flowers are meadow brown and marble white. In fact 33 different species have been seen.

Tilly Whim Caves

The Globe

The high quality building stone embedded within Durlston's cliffs was extensively quarried from the late 18th century onwards, creating huge profits for quarry owners such as John Mowlam and his nephew **George Burt**. But Burt had wider interests and appreciated the natural beauty and richness of this wonderful coastline. In encouraging its enjoyment by others, he built the **castle** as a restaurant, and opened the **Tilly Whim Caves**, old quarry workings in the cliffs, as a public attraction. He also commissioned the **40-ton globe**, standing in an arbour overlooking the sea, and the nearby stone tablets, incised with facts he might have taken from his *Boys Book of Knowledge*.

? *Placed at intervals on the hillside around The Globe are eight benches. What do you suppose they signify?*

GPS WAYPOINTS

SZ 032 773	**B** SZ 029 769
A SZ 034 772	**C** SZ 023 770

3 Tyneham and Gold Down

The finest coastal scenery is not necessarily the most difficult to reach, as this short walk so vividly demonstrates. A dramatic cliff-top path leads to two wonderful bays, where golden sands and tidal pools are certain to make you linger. Ensure, however, that you leave enough time to wander around the abandoned village, its church and school by the car park.

Tyneham's recorded history stretches back to Domesday, but the area was inhabited long before then as the ancient barrows and ring forts on the surrounding hills can testify. Farming and fishing were a way of life for generations, and when mackerel shoals were spotted off the coast, the coastguard would flash a message to Wareham for the dealers to bring their carts. However, all the inhabitants, including the Bonds, who had held the estate since 1683 and lived in their manor house just up the valley, were evacuated in December 1943 when the War Department requisitioned the area and American forces moved in to rehearse their preparations for the D-Day landings.

START Tyneham

ACCESS Tyneham lies within the Lulworth Firing Range, but is open most weekends of the year and daily throughout the peak summer holiday period. Telephone 01929 404 819 to check opening times before you start. *Do not stray outside the marked paths and access areas.*

DISTANCE 2¼ miles (3.6km)

TIME 1¼ hours

PARKING Car park (charge)

ROUTE FEATURES Tracks and coastal paths; unguarded cliffs; moderate climb and steep descent

Follow the track through the car park away from the village, dropping to a junction near toilets at the site of the former Tyneham Farm. Go ahead over a cattle-grid and then bear left on a broad path, defined by yellow-topped posts, that ascends the hillside beyond. The climb is not as arduous as it might appear and, as you gain height, a marvellous view opens along the valley to distract you.

PUBLIC TRANSPORT None

REFRESHMENTS Picnic tables beside car park

PUBLIC TOILETS Near car park

ORDNANCE SURVEY MAP Explorer OL15 (Purbeck & South Dorset)

Tyneham church

Have a look inside the village **schoolhouse**, which has been restored to show how it looked in the years before the war. With only a single classroom, the teacher must have had her work cut out, teaching several different age groups at the same time. Yet, the former inhabitants have fond memories of their days here, as the many interesting recollections displayed around the walls demonstrate.

A At the top, cross a stile and climb right to a second stile. Over that, the onward path, signed to Worbarrow, undulates easily along Gold Down, the westward view bounded by distant Weymouth and the Isle of Portland. Shortly, the descent steepens, dropping to a narrow neck of land separating Pondfield from the main sweep of Worbarrow Bay.

B A gravel track leads back inland above the eastern corner of Worbarrow Bay. After ½ mile (800m) look for a path marked off

Pondfield below Worbarrow Tout

? *How much did it cost to have a telephone in your home before the war?*

Across Worbarrow Bay to the Tout

The area has continued in military use since the end of the Second World War, serving as an **artillery training** range. The occupation has brought its advantages, however, for the land has remained relatively undisturbed and spared the intensive farming practices of the past 60 years. Wildflowers, many of them now becoming quite rare, proliferate in the natural springy turf of the coastal downs. Their presence encourages a wealth of insect life, which in turn supports an abundant variety of birds.

on the left, which drops through the woodland of Tyneham Gwyle, returning you to the picnic area and car park.

GPS WAYPOINTS

SY 881 803   **B** SY 871 797
A SY 883 796

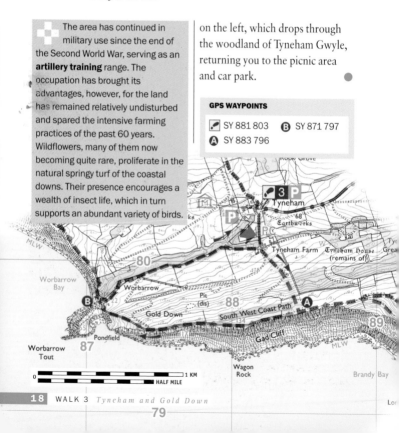

Wareham Forest

START Sika car park
DISTANCE 2½ miles (4km)
TIME 1¼ hours
PARKING Forest car park
ROUTE FEATURES
Woodland paths and
trails; paths may be
muddy after rain

Covering an extensive area of former heath, Wareham Forest is not all trees. It contains a surprising number of different habitats that support a wide range of both plant and animal life. Take a field guide with you on this easy stroll, to help identify some of the many flowers, trees and birds you will spot along the way.

Leave the car park by a large wooden post at its south east corner marking the start of the Sika Trail. A path through the trees leads to a broad crossing track,

Early autumn colours in Wareham Forest

Wareham Forest was begun in the 1930s, the Forestry Commission densely planting fast-growing timber on what had formerly been open, sandy heath. However, the policies of recent years have emphasised a balance between commercial and environmental issues, and the forest now contains a range of species. Although the most commonly planted is the Corsican pine, look more closely and you will also find Scots, Monteray, maritime and bishop's pines too.

PUBLIC TRANSPORT Bus service past car park
REFRESHMENTS Picnic tables beside car park, Headless Woman Inn nearby
(½ mile/800m)
PUBLIC TOILETS None
ORDNANCE SURVEY MAP Explorer OL15 (Purbeck & South Dorset)

where you should turn right, soon passing one of several seats, strategically placed to take advantage of the views or simply enjoy the quietness of the forest. Go ahead at a crossing, but at the next major junction, walk right. Over a rise, the way is joined by another track from the left. Continue a little farther to the forest margin.

Ⓐ At a junction there go left, the way shortly losing height and later turning left into a wide, shallow valley. Following the plantation edge, the track offers a fine view across the marsh to the eastern part of the forest occupying the higher ground on the flanks of Great Ovens Hill.

The forest supports a range of **wildlife**, including two of Britain's rarest reptiles, the smooth snake and the sand lizard, which inhabit the sandy heaths. Come at dawn or dusk and you might spot the sika deer, originally introduced by the landed gentry into deer parks, but now naturalised and favouring the wetter parts of the heath. Among the many birds to look out for are crossbills, Dartford warblers and nightjars.

? *Do you know how to distinguish pine trees from other conifers?*

Across the marshes to Great Ovens Hill

B Eventually, when you reach a crossroads where a track leads away over the bog, keep ahead to a second junction, a little farther on. There, go right, remaining on the periphery of the trees. Not far beyond, however, look for a narrower path leading left off the main track, indicated by a red-topped marker.

C Turn in and walk beside a boggy wetland, colonised by natural woodland trees. Where the path subsequently forks, bear left, rising to higher, drier ground and back into the plantation to meet a main track. Turn right and then, almost immediately, go left to continue climbing through the trees. The way soon reaches a level clearing. Walk ahead to find another main track, and follow it right, back to the car park.

At the edge of Wareham Forest

GPS WAYPOINTS

✏ SY 906 893		**B** SY 914 899
A SY 916 891		**C** SY 912 901

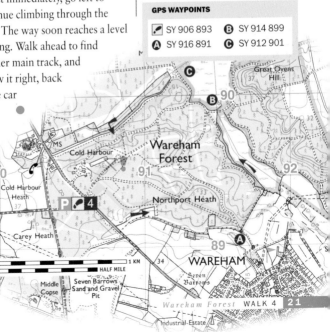

5 Cerne Abbas and its Giant

START Giant View, Cerne Abbas

DISTANCE 2¾ miles (4.4km)

TIME 1¾ hours

PARKING Giant View car park

ROUTE FEATURES Mainly field paths; steep climb; paths may be muddy after rain

No visit to Dorset would be complete without a visit to the country's most famous turf-cut figure, the Cerne Abbas Giant. It is best seen from Giant View, where the walk begins. After wandering around the hill on which it lies, the walk drops past medieval monastic remains and the parish church into the lovely village, nestling below.

🐾 Follow the minor lane off the main road at the southern end of the car park. Go left at the first turning and descend past a picnic area to cross Kettle Bridge. At a junction before Abbey Pottery turn left to a barn and then right, signed 'Giant Hill'. Where the track then immediately divides, go right on a path winding through undergrowth and trees, climbing to a gate and junction of paths.

❓ How many pubs used to stand in the village?

The Cerne Abbas Giant

PUBLIC TRANSPORT Bus service to Cerne Abbas

REFRESHMENTS Picnic area above Kettle Bridge and choice of pubs and tearooms in village

PUBLIC TOILETS In Cerne Abbas

CHILDREN'S PLAY AREA In Cerne Abbas

ORDNANCE SURVEY MAP Explorer 117 (Cerne Abbas & Bere Regis)

The origins of the **Giant** are lost in time, and although not recorded before 1694, tradition assigns him to Roman or even Celtic times. Standing 180 ft (54.9m) tall and brandishing a 120-ft (36.6-m) club, he is thought to represent either a Celtic warrior god or the Roman deity Hercules. His presence may be linked to prehistoric earthworks higher up the hill, where spring maypole dancing perpetuated an association with ancient fertility rites.

The abbey guesthouse

Ⓐ Bear left up steps and then again left, still directed to Giant Hill. After another short pull, the way runs easily below the Giant's feet, just visible above. Continue up the valley, then where the track later splits, bear right to rise along the slope. Farther on, the way climbs more purposefully through scrub before easing across open ground to a stile at the top. A sign, 'Wessex Ridgeway', points across the field beyond to a junction by a barn.

GPS WAYPOINTS

📷 ST 662 016	Ⓒ ST 668 016
Ⓐ ST 666 015	Ⓓ ST 665 013
Ⓑ ST 671 026	Ⓔ ST 664 011

B Go right, following a bridleway to a gate at the far side of the hill. Turn right again, passing through more gates to descend beside the top edge of the field. Through another gate, continue down, now with the fence on your left.

C Approaching the bottom, take the second path marked off on the right, signed 'Abbey and Village'. Over a stile, the way crosses an open meadow, passing ridges and hollows where the abbey once stood. At the far side, follow a wall on your left to a gate into a cemetery. Have a look at St Augustine's Well, over to the left, before leaving the cemetery onto Abbey Street.

First established in 978, the **abbey** was re-founded a century later as a Benedictine house and prospered until the Dissolution in 1539. The great abbey church and most of the monastic buildings have since disappeared, the stone being reused in the village buildings. What remains, however, is impressive: a **15th-century gatehouse**, the guesthouse and part of a tithe barn.

D First, have a look at the gatehouse and guesthouse, which lie to the right and then return along Abbey Street past St Mary's Church into the village. At the end of the street, go right walking as far

Dedicated to St Mary the Virgin, the **church** was begun in the 13th century and occupies the site traditionally associated with St Augustine. Several stories describe his arrival and discovery of the nearby spring, which had been revealed to him in a vision and still flows today. Augustine baptised the villagers in its silver waters and remained there to spend the rest of his life as a hermit.

as the New Inn and turn right into Duck Street.

E Almost immediately, leave along an alley on the right, Mill Lane. Beyond the old mill, continue by a stream, crossing higher up and shortly reaching Kettle Bridge. Turn left and retrace your outward steps to the car park at Giant View.

Enjoying afternoon tea in the village

Kimmeridge Bay and Clavell Tower

6

START Kimmeridge
DISTANCE 2¾ miles (4.4km)
TIME 1¾ hours
PARKING Car park beside lane, north east of Kimmeridge
ROUTE FEATURES Field paths and quiet lanes; steep climb to tower and exposed cliff edge

A shallow valley falls below Kimmeridge to the coast, where it breaks the cliffs to form a delightful sheltered bay. After a short but steep climb to Clavell Tower, rewarded by spectacular views, the return follows a quiet lane from the head of the beach through the charming village with its thatched stone cottages.

From the car park, turn right to find a waymark on the left opposite a junction. Over a stile, walk downhill towards the village, leaving the bottom of the field by the church.

Ⓐ Pass through the churchyard to the lane beyond and turn right, following a track past cottages, signed 'Range Walks and Kimmeridge Bay'. Through a gate, turn left beside a fence, continuing beyond its end to the far corner by a clump of trees. Over a stile beside the left-hand gate, keep ahead at the field edge and then around left

at the far side to reach the opposite corner. Through a gate, carry on across the subsequent fields, now with the boundary on your left, eventually emerging onto a tarmac track.

Cattle graze in the fields around Kimmeridge

PUBLIC TRANSPORT None
REFRESHMENTS Café in village
PUBLIC TOILETS Above Kimmeridge Bay
CHILDREN'S PLAY AREA In village
ORDNANCE SURVEY MAP Explorer OL15 (Purbeck & South Dorset)

Now deceptively peaceful, the bay has been the site of industry for hundreds of years. Celtic Britons quarried the black **Kimmeridge shale**, carving from it amulets and other ornaments, a craft that continued during Roman times. From the late 16th century, the shale was dug for other purposes. John Clavell Smedmore used it to make alum, a chemical much demanded by the tanning and dying industries. Having a high bituminous content, the shale could also be burnt and served as fuel for salt and glass works established in the bay. During the 19th century, a distillation plant was set up to extract gas from the shale, which was then exported to illuminate the streets of Paris. More recently, oil has been discovered, and if you look across the bay, you will see a 'nodding donkey' above the cliffs.

Looking across Kimmeridge Bay to Clavell Tower

C Turn right down towards the beach, but before reaching the bottom, look for the Coast Path signed off through the trees on the left. A steep, stepped path climbs the cliffs, leading to Clavell Tower, which overlooks the bay.

D After savouring the view, retrace your steps to the junction opposite the toilet block **C**, but now bear right, following a narrow tarmac track back to the village. You can avoid some of the lane along a parallel path on the left, which begins just beyond a toll booth. Carry on through the village to the church and then retrace your outward route up the field behind to the car park. ●

Footpath by Kimmeridge Coppice

B Go left, but leave again after 100 yds (90m), bearing right along the bottom edge of an open meadow used as a car park. Follow the top of the cliffs around to reach a junction by a toilet block.

Built in 1830 by the Reverend John Richards, the **tower** takes its name from the Clavells who lived at nearby Smedmore House and developed the first industries in the bay. Conceived as a folly, it later served as a lookout for a nearby lifeboat station, but was subsequently damaged when fire broke out. A ruin for many years, it has recently been moved back from the eroding cliff edge, rebuilt and restored by the Landmark Trust and converted into self-catering accommodation.

Inside the church porch is a strangely carved stone, what was its purpose?

Looking west across Kimmeridge Bay towards Broad Bench

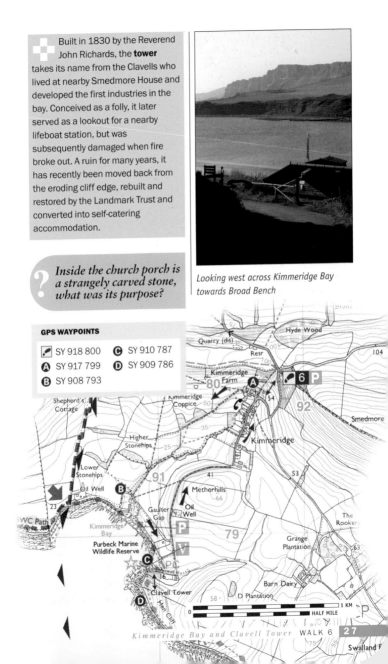

GPS WAYPOINTS

📏 SY 918 800	**C** SY 910 787	
A SY 917 799	**D** SY 909 786	
B SY 908 793		

7 Osmington White Horse

START Osmington
DISTANCE 3¼ miles (5.2km)
TIME 1½ hours
PARKING Roadside parking by the church in Osmington
ROUTE FEATURES Field tracks and paths; moderate climb

Thatched cottages and rambling roses line Osmington's main street, which leads onto the downs behind where there are fine views across the surrounding countryside. Winding back above Saxon field systems, the walk returns to the village, whose pub offers a tempting selection of dishes to round off the day.

🖉 Follow Church Lane down through Osmington past the church, walking ahead at a junction, signed to the White Horse. Beyond the houses, the way degrades to a track, continuing between high hedges that, in summer, unfortunately, tend to obscure your view of the hillside figure. Not to worry, though, for you will get a better view of it later on in the walk.

A The way breaks clear at the foot of the bank, turning to ease the gradient of the climb across the face of the slope. As you gain height, a superb panorama opens up to the coast, a wide sweep around Weymouth to Portland Bill dominating the scene to the west. Levelling at the top, the track continues ahead to a junction.

B The white horse lies below the bank a little farther to the west, but the onward route lies sharp right, signed to Poxwell. A level track leads easily along the crest of a broad ridge, allowing views to the north as well as to the Channel. Keep going, later passing a barn down to the left before rising on a wide, grassy drove towards a transmitter mast. Just before it, however, the way bends to the right and, once through two gates,

PUBLIC TRANSPORT Bus service to Osmington
REFRESHMENTS Sunray Inn at Osmington (outdoor family area and playground)
PUBLIC TOILETS None
ORDNANCE SURVEY MAP Explorer OL15 (Purbeck & South Dorset)

The **church** is dedicated to St Osmund, who was appointed Bishop of Salisbury in the 11th century and founded the first cathedral there. The **village**, however, is much older than the church and is mentioned in a 10th-century document as forming part of a grant of land to Milton Abbey by King Athelstan. The figure on the hillside above Osmington is unique in that it is the only **white horse** among several in the country that bears a rider on its back, which is said to represent King George III, commemorating his visit to Weymouth in 1805.

descends at the right-hand edge of a field. A small mound, seen to the left, is not a barrow (an ancient burial mound), as are many such bumps gracing the tops of the Dorset hills, but in fact a small water reservoir. Carry on in the next field to Pixon Barn, and through a gate there, turn right onto a track to Osmington.

Osmington Church

GPS WAYPOINTS

SY 724 830 **B** SY 718 844
A SY 721 839 **C** SY 735 838

Across the bay to Portland Bill

C Through gates, the track continues at the edge of successive fields, shortly losing height towards the village. Early farmers cut terraces from the slopes below to create strip fields, known as lynchets. Across the valley is a view of the white horse. Approaching Osmington, the track becomes enclosed, and drops past cottages to end at Church Lane. The Sunray Inn lies up to the left, and the church is ahead and round to the left.

A famous 19th-century visitor to Osmington was the Suffolk-born artist **John Constable**, regarded as one of the greatest English landscape painters. He and his wife, Maria, spent part of their honeymoon as guests of John Fisher, who was vicar in the village. Constable was much taken by the place, and produced a number of sketches and paintings of the nearby coast and countryside, but never returned to visit his friend, the vicarage being too small to accommodate both their families.

The village church is dedicated to St Osmund. Where can you find a likeness of him?

Osmington White Horse

Abbotsbury

8

START Chesil Beach, near Abbotsbury Gardens
DISTANCE 3½ miles (5.6km)
TIME 2 hours
PARKING Beach car park (charge)
ROUTE FEATURES Field tracks and paths; moderate climbs

The largest single physical feature in Dorset is Chesil Beach, a 17-mile (27.4km) bank of shingle stretching from West Bay to the Isle of Portland. There is a good view along it from this walk, which climbs onto Chapel Hill above Abbotsbury before dropping to the Swannery, a great favourite with children, at the head of the Fleet Nature Reserve.

Walk through the car park towards the shingle bank to meet the coast path, and turn left. At first the going is hard work on the loose pebbles behind the beach, but the path soon becomes firmer, turning to the left around the base of a hill, whose grassy slopes were terraced into strip fields by ancient farmers. Pass a path on the right, signed to the Swannery, and continue to a junction of tracks.

A Bear right, signed 'Village and Chapel Hill', passing through a gate and continue to arrive at a second junction. Again bear right, walking a little farther to reach a barn, where you should go through a kissing gate on the right, signed 'St Catherine's Chapel'.

Standing some 280 ft (85m) above the sea, **St Catherine's Chapel** has long served seafarers as a landmark on this dangerous coast. It was built around the beginning of the 15th century as a pilgrim's chapel for the nearby monastery and is constructed entirely of stone that had to be hauled up the hillside from the quarries below.

PUBLIC TRANSPORT Bus service to Swannery (alternative start)
REFRESHMENTS Cafés next to car park (seasonal), Swannery and nearby Abbotsbury Gardens, choice of pubs and tearooms in Abbotsbury
PUBLIC TOILETS Adjacent to car park and at Swannery
ORDNANCE SURVEY MAP Explorer OL15 (Purbeck & South Dorset)

B Bear right to climb the hill, passing to the left of a wall corner, then continue to bear right uphill. Keep going to reach St Catherine's Chapel on the summit from where there is a superb panorama.

Separated from the sea by the shingle bar is the **Fleet**, the largest tidal lagoon in Britain and now protected as an important nature reserve. **Swans** have been kept in the pools at its northern end since at least 1393, originally providing food, down and quill pens for the monks of St Peter's Abbey, a Benedictine community founded in 1023.

St Catherine's Chapel

? *What is a young swan called?*

GPS WAYPOINTS

SY 560 846	**C** SY 572 848
A SY 570 850	**D** SY 576 845
B SY 575 851	

Thatched cottages in Abbotsbury

C Retrace your steps down the hill to the bottom kissing-gate **B**, but instead of passing through, turn sharp right to follow a path back beside a wall around the base of the hill. When you reach a signpost, keep straight ahead over a bridge towards the Swannery, with a wall left. Walk down to cross a wall stile beneath some trees. Turn right – the entrance to the Swannery lies a short distance down the lane.

D Retrace your steps up the lane from the Swannery, but immediately past the café, turn off left onto a permissive path to the coast path and Tropical Gardens. Cross a stile into a field, and keep ahead to cross another. Continue below the southern flank of Chapel Hill. Later follow the path through a gate; the way loses height beside a fence, eventually meeting the outward track. Turn left and walk back to the car park.

Chesil Beach, whose name derives from an Old English word meaning 'shingle', is thought to have formed at the end of the last Ice Age from debris deposited by glacial meltwater. As the English Channel subsequently flooded, powerful currents and storms forced the rocks into a line along the coast, smoothing and sorting them as the process continued. Curiously, the pebbles are evenly graded along the beach, and so consistent is the variation, that it is said 18th-century smugglers landing illicit cargoes at night could tell exactly where they were from the size of the stones on the beach.

Feeding time at the Swannery

9 The forts on Hod and Hambledon Hills

START	Nutcombe Wood
DISTANCE	3¾ miles (6km)
TIME	2¼ hours
PARKING	Car park south east of Child Okeford
ROUTE FEATURES	Grassy paths and tracks; initial steep climb; paths may be slippery when wet

Seen from a distance, these hills present a formidable prospect, a feature exploited by Iron Age tribes who threw up mighty defences around their summits. Yet the walk is less strenuous than might first appear and conveniently passes close to the village of Iwerne Courtney (known locally as Shroton), where a short detour to the pub makes an ideal lunch break.

Hod Hill's fort

🖊 A path, marked as a bridleway, rises through the trees behind the car park to a gate above. Continue climbing beside Nutcombe Wood on your right and, beyond a gate at the top, pass between steep grassy banks of the earthwork enclosures surmounting Hod Hill. Continue in a diagonal line across the more-or-less level centre, passing out of the opposite corner of the smaller Roman fort about halfway along.

Ⓐ At the far corner of the enclosure, the path falls through a gap in the defences to a gate. However, immediately before the gate, turn left to find a path that courses the base of the embankment. After some 300 yds (274m), drop through a gate on the right to a gravel track below and follow it away to the left.

PUBLIC TRANSPORT Bus service to Iwerne Courtney (alternative start)
REFRESHMENTS Cricketers' Inn at nearby Iwerne Courtney
PUBLIC TOILETS None
ORDNANCE SURVEY MAP Explorer 118 (Shaftesbury & Cranborne Chase)

Although its earthwork defences may not appear as impressive as the more famous Maiden Castle, the **Iron Age fort** on Hod Hill is actually the largest in Dorset, enclosing 54 acres (22 ha) and once containing a village of some 250 circular huts. High concentric embankments, each protected by a deep ditch encircling the summit of a naturally steep hill, were imposing defences and served the inhabitants well until the Romans arrived around AD44. Their disciplined training and practised strategies made short work of any resistance the Britons could mount, and the fort was quickly taken. Its strategic importance overlooking the Stour and Iwerne valleys was used to advantage by the occupying forces, who built their own, smaller fort within the north west corner of the enclosure. Both infantry and cavalry were stationed there, a force of some 700 men and 250 horses.

B Just before reaching a gate onto a road at the end, take a path on the left that winds through the trees and through two gates to emerge into a field. Walk down by the right-hand hedge, to leave at the bottom corner onto a lane.

C Cross to a gate opposite and carry on ahead, rising at the edge of a meadow. Through a gate by overhead power cables, a path descends through scrub to more hillside grazing. Keep on down by its edge to a crossing of paths at the end, there bearing right to continue on a marked bridleway with a wood, The Shrubbery, on your right.

> **?** *How many rows of defending ramparts surround the Hambledon Hill fort?*

Cattle grazing Hod Hill's ramparts

Looking back to Iwerne Courtney

D The track shortly rises to a junction, where, through a gate ahead, it continues downfield to Iwerne Courtney. (*However, as the onward route lies to the left, if you go into the village, return to this point afterwards.*) The track to Hambledon Hill climbs left along a broad ridge and, as you gain height, there are views both to Hod Hill on the left and to your next objective, which appears ahead to the right. Carry on to reach a junction by a trig point.

E Access to Hambledon Hill is through a gate on the right, and you can wander freely over the site to explore the ancient fortifications and enjoy the fine views over the surrounding countryside. The way back, however, lies to the left, along a contained path that passes the older Neolithic earthworks. Through a gate at the end, follow the left-hand edge of successive fields down until you reach a barn.

The crescent shape of **Hambledon Hill** allows a fine view across the fort's western defences. Although it looks more imposing than that on Hod Hill, historians believe that, after seeing the futility of their neighbours' attempts to withstand the Roman onslaught, the occupants surrendered their position without a fight. Iron Age tribes were not the first to settle here, and the hill to the south east bears traces of an extensive Neolithic or New Stone Age settlement. However, now some 5,000 years old, they are not all that easy to distinguish for the unpractised eye.

F Immediately past the barn, turn right and continue your descent, the way now steepening to the bottom of the field. Emerging onto a lane, turn right and walk back to the car park. ●

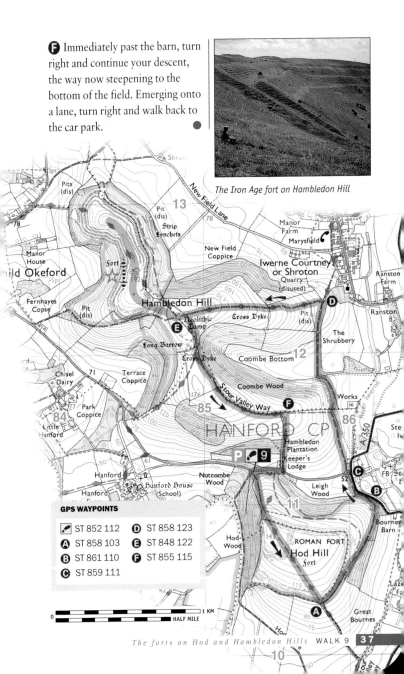

The Iron Age fort on Hambledon Hill

GPS WAYPOINTS

🗺 ST 852 112	**D** ST 858 123	
A ST 858 103	**E** ST 848 122	
B ST 861 110	**F** ST 855 115	
C ST 859 111		

0   1 KM
HALF MILE

10 *Langdon Hill and Golden Cap*

START North eastern corner of Langdon Hill (off A35)

DISTANCE 4 miles (6.4 km)

TIME 2½ hours

PARKING National Trust car park

ROUTE FEATURES Woodland and field paths; steep climbs and descent; exposed cliffs

Beginning around a wooded hill, this splendid walk leads onto Golden Cap, a National Trust estate important, not only for its prehistoric remains, but also for the plant and insect life of its meadows and hedges. At Seatown, there is a delightful beach and the opportunity of a pub lunch before climbing back across the fields.

Walk to the top of the parking area and turn right along a broad woodland track that encircles the upper part of Langdon Hill. Ignore a path forking right just after rounding the northern point and continue along the hill's western flank, where breaks in the trees allow a view to Lyme Regis. At the southern corner, leave the track, turning first sharply right onto a descending path and then left where it splits, dropping onto the end of Pettycrate Lane.

Ⓐ Through a gate to the right, bear right across a field to reach another gate part-way along its far boundary. Following a sign to St Gabriel's, carry on at the edge of the next field, shortly reaching a stile.

The path at the bottom of Golden Cap

PUBLIC TRANSPORT Bus service to Seatown (alternative start)

REFRESHMENTS Anchor Inn and snack bar at Seatown

PUBLIC TOILETS At Seatown

ORDNANCE SURVEY MAP Explorer 116 (Lyme Regis & Bridport)

The view towards Chesil Beach from Golden Cap

B Over that, keep left, a waymark directing you by the fence across the side of the hill towards the Coast Path. Turn left when you

At 626 ft (191m) above sea level, **Golden Cap** is the highest point along the Channel coast. Its name derives from the warm yellow sandstone, which is exposed at the top of the cliff. However, the cliffs below are composed of crumbling blue lias clays, making them unstable and prone to frequent landslip, and it has been calculated that the cliffs are receding at the rate of three ft (91cm) each year. Yet even this has its advantages, for the clay is rich in fossils, which are constantly being exposed as the cliffs fall into the sea. The most spectacular find was a 35-ft (10.7-m) ichthyosaur discovered in 1986, although more common specimens consist of small ammonites and belemnites.

GPS WAYPOINTS

📷	SY 411 930	**C**	SY 407 922
A	SY 410 923	**D**	SY 419 917
B	SY 405 923	**E**	SY 420 921

reach another stile and climb a steep, zigzagging path through bracken to the top of Golden Cap.

C Beyond the trig point, a steep path descends the hill at the far side, dropping through a kissing-gate into a field at the bottom. Turn right following its edge, the sign directing you along the Coast Path to Seatown. Steeply descend the fields towards the village, crossing a couple of stiles as you descend. Lower down, you are directed left because of landslip, the way passing through a gate and then ahead to a stile into a small copse. Beyond that, cross a crop field and carry on beside a garden to emerge onto a lane. The beach lies a short distance to the right.

D Retrace your steps along the lane from the beach, continuing up

Seatown's beach

The Dorset coastline has always been hazardous to shipping, a fact vividly demonstrated by the massive **anchor** on display outside the Anchor Inn. It was found by a fisherman trawling off the coast in 1985, and came from the *Hope of Amsterdam*, a Dutch treasure ship that foundered on Chesil Beach in January 1748. Although the crew managed to save themselves, the ship was wrecked and, as word of its cargo spread, thousands of people flocked to the beach in search of gold and silver.

the hill past the point where you first joined it, until you reach a track signed off on the left past Seahill House to Langdon Hill.

E There follows a gentle climb along Pettycrate Lane. Where it forks, branch left, later passing through a gate and on below the wooded slopes of Langdon Hill, soon to pass a stile on the left. Keep going beyond it for another 150 yds (137m), then turn right on a narrow path that climbs through a gap in a wire fence into the trees above. Emerging onto a broad woodland track at the top, turn right and walk back to the car park.

? *What is unusual about the memorial stone to the Earl of Antrim on top of Golden Cap?*

Studland and Old Harry Rocks

START Studland
DISTANCE 4 miles (6.4km)
TIME 2½ hours
PARKING South Beach National Trust car park (charge)
ROUTE FEATURES Downland tracks; moderate climb; unguarded cliff-top paths

11

Although involving some climbing, this walk is not overly demanding. From the attractive village of Studland, it follows the cliffs to Handfast Point, below which is one of Dorset's most impressive coastal rock formations. Returning across the downs, the ramble finishes past the finest surviving example of early Norman architecture in the county.

Turn right out of the car park and walk down past the Bankes Arms. Just beyond a toilet block, go left, signed to Old Harry along a rising track. After a short climb, the gradient eases above the cliffs, giving a fine view back over South Beach as you walk on ahead towards the point. From the headland there is a grandstand view to the massive detached stacks that are Old Harry Rocks.

? *Where in Studland will you find a violin, a bomb, a supersonic plane, and a butterfly?*

However, do not get too close to the cliff edge, for it is a sheer drop below.

A After enjoying the unsurpassed views, continue on around the coast, again gaining height along the rising cliffs. The way passes above the Pinnacles, slender isolated fingers of white chalk, shortly bringing you to a fence higher up. Remain on the outside and then bear right at a fork higher up, signed 'Ulwell', to continue climbing by the fence to a gate. Carry on through that and past a trig point just beyond.

PUBLIC TRANSPORT Bus service to Studland
REFRESHMENTS Pub, farm tearoom and Joe's café (South Beach) at Studland
PUBLIC TOILETS In Studland
ORDNANCE SURVEY MAP Explorer OL15 (Purbeck & South Dorset)

Old Harry Rocks, and the other stacks along the coast, were once part of the cliffs, but became separated as the waves, exploiting weaknesses in the rock, created caves, which subsequently collapsed. The sea continues to worry at their bases, and one day, they too will tumble into the waves, adding to the rubble below the cliffs.

B With the steepest part of the climb now over, the way undulates gently ahead along the spine of Ballard Down. Over to the left is the seaside town of Swanage and on the right, Studland Bay. To the north west, lies the vast expanse of Poole Harbour, one of the largest natural harbours in the world and in the middle of which sits the Brownsea Island Nature Reserve. Beyond a gate carry on along the ridge until you reach a four-finger signpost.

C From this point, you can extend the walk by continuing west along the ridge for another ¾ mile (1.2km) where, just beyond the crest, is a stone obelisk erected in 1892 to commemorate the installation of running water in Swanage. However, the return to Studland lies to the right along a developing track, which heads north east to find an easy line of descent across the flank of the hill. Through a gate at the bottom, turn

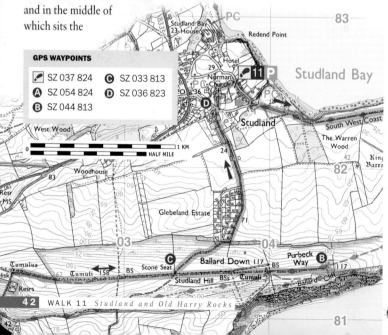

GPS WAYPOINTS

✎ SZ 037 824	**C**	SZ 033 813
A SZ 054 824	**D**	SZ 036 823
B SZ 044 813		

right onto a tarmac track. After winding around behind some houses, it eventually passes Manor Farm, which makes a convenient stop for tea, before emerging on the bend of a lane opposite the village's cross.

D Bear left past the cross and, where the lane then bends right, go ahead following a sign to the church. Continue beyond the building and then turn right, crossing the churchyard to leave by a kissing-gate. As you pass the northern side of the church look up to see a row of figures carved on the corbels below the roof. A contained path then skirts a small paddock, regaining the road beside the car park entrance. ●

Pinnacle

St Nicholas is one of many churches bearing that dedication along the Dorset coast. A 4th-century bishop of Myra, now in Turkey, his pious life, generosity to the poor and miraculous deeds prompted his adoption as the patron saint of pawnbrokers, sailors and children as well as by two countries and several cities. The custom of giving presents in his name first developed among Dutch Protestants, to whom he is known as Sinte Klaas. The church itself is Norman, but is a rebuilding of a much earlier chapel, established towards the end of the 7th century and later plundered by the Danes.

12 Hardy's Cottage and Lower Bockhampton

START Thorncombe Wood
DISTANCE 4¼ miles (6.8km)
TIME 2½ hours
PARKING Car park beside Thorncombe Wood
ROUTE FEATURES Woodland and field paths; paths may be muddy after rain

An enjoyable ramble through woodland, heath and farmland, the countryside where Thomas Hardy spent his childhood days. Passing the cottages where the author was born and the wonderful gardens and rare farm breeds collection at Kingston Maurward, this walk offers everything for a full day out.

Hardy's Egdon Heath

🥾 A path to Hardy's Cottage leaves the car park beside an information display. After a short climb, the way levels to a junction **A**, where the cottage is signed to the left. Go left again at the end to the entrance.

B Retrace your steps to **A** and turn left. Twisting through the

? *Which of Hardy's novels were written in the family cottage at Higher Bockhampton?*

PUBLIC TRANSPORT Bus service to Lower Bockhampton (alternative start)
REFRESHMENTS Restaurant for visitors to Kingston Maurward Gardens
PUBLIC TOILETS None
ORDNANCE SURVEY MAP Explorer OL15 (Purbeck & South Dorset) or Explorer 117 (Cerne Abbas & Bere Regis)

Hardy was born in 1840, and grew up in the area before pursuing a career as an architect. Ill health forced his return to Dorset where he began writing, drawing his inspiration from the countryside and its characters. His plots used real places, although many of the names he gave them were of his own invention; Puddletown Heath, above the cottage, was Egdon Heath and nearby Dorchester, where he attended school, became Casterbridge.

trees, the path leads to the Swallet Holes, massive natural depressions in the ground. There, go left again, passing them to an iron fence, through which the path climbs onto more open heath. At a fork just past an information panel, bear left beside Rushy Pool to reach a

track and, over a stile to the left, go immediately right across a second stile, signed 'Norris Mill'.

C Branch left where the path then forks, following the course of a Roman road. At the far end, bend left to meet a crossing track and there turn right. Keep to the main path when it later curves right, to drop steeply through encroaching rhododendrons. As the gradient eases, carry on ahead past two trails off left, until eventually the track itself turns sharply left.

D There, leave and go ahead on a narrow path through more rhododendrons, crossing a couple of stiles to emerge in a field. Strike out to find a stile at the far side,

Hardy's Cottage

Swan beside the River Frome

just left of a house which comes into view beyond.

E Cross a lane to a track opposite, beside the house, and follow it to a fork in front of barns at Norris Mill Farm. Bear right over a stile and through a gate to walk away, cresting a rise to a stile and field. Take a shallow right diagonal across, making for Duddle Farm, visible in the middle distance. Over stiles separated by a plank bridge, keep straight ahead across the next field to meet a stile and track by the farm.

F Cross to a stile opposite and continue ahead across a narrow paddock and the field beyond. At the far side, over another stile, bear left around the base of higher ground, parallel to a bushy hedge concealing a stream. A developing grassy track leads to a cottage by Bhompston Farm, where a gravel track leads past more cottages to a junction.

G Walk ahead through a gate towards Lower Bockhampton, but where the track then bends right, cross a stile into a field on the left and walk down to its far bottom corner. Beyond a kissing-gate, continue across an open pasture, making for Kingston Dairy House. Carry on through the farmyard to a lane.

H Turn right and then left, signed 'Higher Kingston'; the lane leading into the grounds of Kingston Maurward College. Bear right in front of the old manor house, and then beyond the former stables, head left, the way signed 'Higher Bockhampton'. Through gates,

The old schoolhouse in Lower Bockhampton

Hardy set Lower Bockhampton's **Elizabethan manor house** in his first published novel, *Desperate Remedies*, in which it became the home of Aenaes Manston. The nearby **Kingston Maurward**, whose gardens are open to the public, was built at the beginning of the 18th century by George Pitt, after he acquired the estate on his marriage to Laura, last of the Greys who had held the old manor.

walk along a track and then at the field edge to come out at a lane.

❶ Follow the track opposite for about 20 yds (18m) and then strike right across a crop field, again signed 'Higher Bockhampton'. Through a gate at the far side, bear right, on a rising track towards a barn and then go right at the top to emerge onto a lane. Turn left and then right, following the lane back to the car park. ●

GPS WAYPOINTS

🖋 SY 725 921		**E** SY 763 912
A SY 726 922		**F** SY 731 908
B SY 728 925		**G** SY 725 907
C SY 730 921		**H** SY 720 908
D SY 735 916		**I** SY 717 916

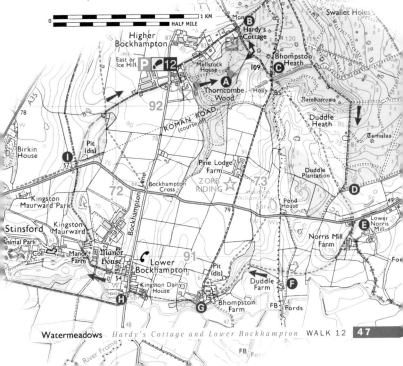

Watermeadows *Hardy's Cottage and Lower Bockhampton* WALK 12

13 Clouds Hill and Moreton

START Bovington Heath (north of Bovington Camp)

DISTANCE 4¼ miles (6.8km)

TIME 2½ hours

PARKING Roadside car park

ROUTE FEATURES Woodland tracks and paths

Thomas Edward Lawrence, better known to many as 'Lawrence of Arabia', was one of the most outstanding men of his age, a man of vision and determination whose life has become legendary. This walk explores the area to which he retired before his tragic death in 1935 after a motorcycle accident.

From the car park, follow a wooded footpath north between the tank training course and the road. A short distance along, look for a memorial stone on the left, placed near the spot where Lawrence was fatally injured. In a little while, the path turns away from the tank run to end at a road, passing behind Clouds Hill, the small house that Lawrence bought when stationed at Bovington. Turn left along the verge to a crossroads.

> **?** *What was the make of T E Lawrence's motorcycle?*

Moreton Plantation

PUBLIC TRANSPORT Bus service to nearby Bovington Camp
REFRESHMENTS Tearoom at Moreton and café at nearby tank museum
PUBLIC TOILETS None
ORDNANCE SURVEY MAP Explorer OL15 (Purbeck & South Dorset)

Of Anglo-Irish descent and born at Tremadoc in Wales in 1888, **Lawrence** went to Oxford where he studied modern history. His association with the Arabic world began at the age of 23, when he embarked on a 1,100 mile (1,770km) trek through Palestine and Syria before working there as an archaeologist. With the outbreak of the First World War, Lawrence's knowledge of the Arab peoples and their language qualified him for work with army intelligence in North Africa, where in 1916 he took up the Arab cause against the Turks. Although successfully leading the Arabs in action, during the negotiations that followed, Lawrence was unable to achieve what he regarded as a proper settlement and, in 1922, retired from the public eye. In an unsuccessful attempt to obtain anonymity, he took the name of John Ross and joined the RAF as an aircraftsman. As T E Shaw, he later enlisted in the Tank Corps at Bovington before finally returning to the RAF, working on the development of rescue boats until his retirement in 1935.

A The entrance to Clouds Hill lies a short distance to the left, but the walk continues along the road (can be busy) ahead for ¼ mile (400m) to the next junction. There, turn left and follow a broad track into the Moreton Plantation. Carry on through the forest for 1¼ miles (2km), ignoring side tracks and paths. Eventually, just beyond a bridge keep right as the track forks in front of a private drive and continue to a ford across the River Frome, a causeway providing a dryshod alternative. Beyond, the way leads to the village, but approaching a road junction, look for a drive on the left that leads to St Nicholas' Church, where Lawrence's funeral service was held and is worth visiting for its fine engraved windows by Sir Laurence Whistler.

Playing beside the ford at Moreton

B Return to the lane and turn left. Ahead, not far beyond the crossroads is the entrance to Moreton Cemetery. Lawrence's grave lies towards the far end.

The tank training is quite spectacular

Following his discharge from the services, Lawrence retired to Clouds Hill, but only months later, died after a motorcycle accident. He had been returning home after posting a letter. The funeral service at **Moreton Church** was attended by many notable people, including Winston Churchill, Lady Astor and Bernard Shaw. **Lawrence's grave** in the nearby cemetery is marked by a simple stone carved by his friend, Eric Kennington.

C Retrace your steps through the village and across the River Frome, continuing beyond the second bridge until you reach a junction, where a track leaves to the right between open fields. Farther on, at a fork, bear left, the way shortly taking you past a cottage and into a wood. Through a barrier, carry on into the trees, soon entering more open heath.

D Where the way then divides, bear left rising into a plantation of pine. At another junction go right, still climbing gently through the trees and eventually reaching a gate and stile at the edge of Bovington's armoured vehicle proving ground. Turn left beside the perimeter fence, soon returning to the road opposite the parking area. ●

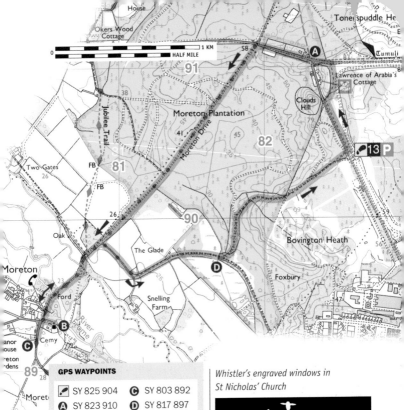

GPS WAYPOINTS

🖊 SY 825 904	Ⓒ SY 803 892
Ⓐ SY 823 910	Ⓓ SY 817 897
Ⓑ SY 805 892	

Whistler's engraved windows in
St Nicholas' Church

Bovington Camp is the home
of the Royal Armoured Corps,
and areas of the forest and heath
around the camp form part of the
training ground. Behind the parking
area is the tank training track, and
you might get a grandstand view as
tank crews are taught to negotiate
obstacles such as the massive
earthen mound opposite. For an even
closer look at tanks, visit the nearby
museum, where you will learn
something of the fascinating history
of armoured warfare.

14 *Wareham*

Cradled within the tidal confluence of the rivers Frome and Piddle, Wareham is almost entirely surrounded by water, and for centuries was a strategic stronghold and important trading place. Passing some of the historic sites within the town, this walk also explores the marshes on its seaward flank, which are an important habitat for birds.

START Church of St Martin's, Wareham
DISTANCE 4¼ miles (6.8km)
TIME 2½ hours
PARKING Several car parks in town (Pay and Display)
ROUTE FEATURES Meadow and riverside paths; paths may be muddy after rain

The earliest evidence of settlement in **Wareham** dates to the Iron Age, although it is from the Saxon period that the town developed as an important port. Its position made it a regular target for parties of raiding Danes and it was taken in 876 by Guthrum. The invaders left, however, after being defeated the next year by Alfred in the sea battle off Swanage. To prevent recapture, Alfred raised the town's **defensive ramparts**, which were reinforced on several occasions during the subsequent centuries and at one time carried a stone wall along their top.

? *How many sides does a hexagon have?*

St Martin's Church stands on the old ramparts, along which the walk begins, following a footpath east from the church. Reaching a street at the bottom, go left and then right before looking for another path signed off on the left. Back on top of the walls, the way sweeps around a grassed open space. Shortly, approaching another street on your right, look for a path on your right and drop down the wooded outer bank to a tarmac track at the bottom.

Ⓐ To the left, the track curves around into the woodland of Bestwall Park, parallel with the

PUBLIC TRANSPORT Bus and rail services to Wareham
REFRESHMENTS Choice of pubs and cafés in town
PUBLIC TOILETS In town
ORDNANCE SURVEY MAP Explorer OL15 (Purbeck & South Dorset)

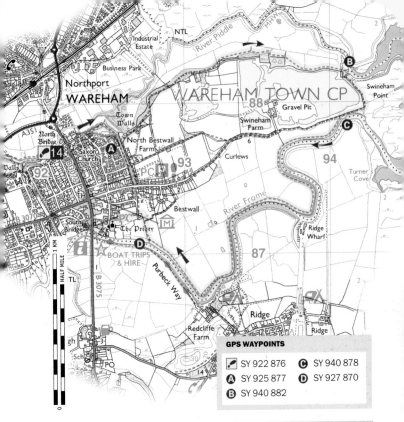

GPS WAYPOINTS

🥾	SY 922 876	**C**	SY 940 878
A	SY 925 877	**D**	SY 927 870
B	SY 940 882		

course of the Piddle, which lies just to the north. Keep ahead across a dirt access track servicing gravel pits, and then branch left when the track forks a little farther on, by North Bestwall House. Where it finally ends, pass through a gate onto the open marsh. Carry on at the edge, at first following an obvious track, and when that later peters out, continue generally ahead parallel, to a fence and hedge.

St Martin's is the oldest surviving church in Dorset and dates from around 1020. From the outside it is a plain building and displays 'long and short' work in its construction, a detail typical of Saxon architecture. Inside, its height is emphasised by the narrowness of the nave, the north aisle having been added later during the Norman period. 12th-century frescoes adorn the chancel, depicting events from the life of St Martin, and in the aisle is Eric Kennington's carved effigy of T E Lawrence in Arabian dress.

The lead font in Lady St Mary's Church

Ⓑ When you eventually reach a metal kissing-gate, go through and take the short raised permissive path immediately on the right. The way continues beyond along a hedged path, bordering a lake. To the left, however, is the open reed marsh, which stretches on to Swineham Point. Shortly, the path turns to meet the River Frome and heads upstream towards the town.

Feeding the ducks opposite the old quay

Ⓒ Not far along, where the path divides above a sluice gate, bear left to follow the sinuous wanderings of the river, whose banks are lined with moored boats. In the distance, beyond the expansive, haunting marsh, Wareham's other ancient church, dedicated to the Lady St Mary, stands as an obvious landmark in the distance.

> **Lady St Mary's Church** was also a Saxon foundation and part of a priory that once lay to the east. The earliest parts disappeared when the church was largely rebuilt in 1842, although the St Edward Chapel, chancel and tower remain from the medieval period. Inside are preserved some early Christian Celtic inscriptions and you will also see two splendid effigies of 13th-century knights. Equally interesting is the hexagonal lead font, thought to have been made in about 1200 and which is said to be unique.

Ⓓ Eventually, the path leaves the water, crossing duckboards to a junction of paths. Turn left on a permissive footpath leading out to a track and there go right and then left, passing through the town's extensive cemetery to reach St Mary's Church. Continue beyond its west end and bear left to the old quay and South Bridge, there joining the main street back through the town centre. ●

St Aldhelm's Head and Worth Matravers

15

START South of Renscombe Farm
DISTANCE 4¼ miles (6.8km)
TIME 2½ hours
PARKING Coastal car park (charge)
ROUTE FEATURES Tracks and field paths; unguarded cliff path; abrupt steep descent and re-ascent, which may be slippery when wet (can be avoided by alternative return)

After passing through picturesque Worth Matravers, where St Nicholas' Church displays fine Norman work, the way continues along the cliffs to St Aldhelm's Head, a beautiful spot on a fine summer's day, offering superb views along the coast. Yet, when winter storms rage, it becomes utterly inhospitable, warranting the solid squat construction of the lonely chapel.

A sign opposite the car park indicates the start of a path, heading east at the field edge towards Worth Matravers. At the far side, follow a track into Weston Farm, bear left past barns and walk out to a lane. Turn right towards the village and, when you reach a junction by the village hall, go left up to St Nicholas' Church.

Ⓐ Carry on past the church to the village pond, there turning right to double back below a small garden. Just beyond, go left along a cottage-lined street, continuing down a path and through a gate at the far end. The path later broadens into a track, descending steadily along a deepening valley towards the coast, eventually passing Winspit Cottage. The terracing you can see on the surrounding hillsides was to enable more land to be cultivated by ox-drawn ploughs. The date of the terraces is debatable but in the 16th century they were used for growing flax.

Ⓑ Approaching a rocky cove, look for a stepped path climbing to the

---

PUBLIC TRANSPORT Bus service to Worth Matravers (alternative start)
REFRESHMENTS Tearoom and pub in Worth Matravers
PUBLIC TOILETS In Worth Matravers
ORDNANCE SURVEY MAP Explorer OL15 (Purbeck & South Dorset)

The fine **Purbeck limestone** was much in demand as a building material, its fine grain allowing it to be polished like marble. Many quarries and underground workings similar to those at Winspit and St Aldhelm's Head operated along the coast. Once cut, and often shaped in the quarry to its required size, the stone was loaded from the cliffs onto small barges for transfer to larger vessels standing offshore or waiting at Swanage. Formerly echoing to the noise of dusty activity, the Winspit quarries have lain deserted since production finished during the mid-1940s.

Sunset at Chapman's Pool

right, which leads around the head of the former Winspit quarries. Beyond, follows an exhilarating walk along the cliff top towards the point. Although the contours obscure a view ahead along this stretch of coast, pause to look back for a splendid picture along the cliffs to the lighthouse on Anvil Point. When you eventually reach a crossing of paths by a marker, go ahead and then left, passing above more quarries, shortly to reach the coastguard station on St Aldhelm's Head.

C *If you wish to avoid the steep descent and climb which lies a little farther round the coast, you can cut the walk short by returning along the bridleway beside St Aldhelm's*

Chapel. However, as this misses some of the finest scenery along this stretch of coast, the best route continues along the coastal path, which at first appears to run in an unbroken line towards Chapman's Pool. The reality is soon dramatically revealed as a deep, steep-sided valley opens before you. But, take your time, both going down and ascending, and you will find it not as bad as it appears. Beyond, the walking is easy again, with an enchanting view into the cove ahead.

D All too soon, the coast walk is over. Shortly after passing a memorial to the Royal Marines, look for a stone sign indicating the path inland to Renscombe. Leaving

95

through a gate, a clear path crosses a couple of fields back to the car park.

●

? *Near the coastguard station on St Aldhelm's Head is a sculpture, at first sight appearing as a beacon, but what is it?*

GPS WAYPOINTS

🖉 SY 964 773		🅲 SY 960 754	
🅐 SY 972 774		🅳 SY 958 768	
🅑 SY 976 761			

St Aldhelm was the first Bishop of Sherborne and lived during the 7th century. It is believed that the **12th-century chapel** is built on an early Christian site, possibly a chapel or hermitage. Legend credits its foundation to a Norman knight, who watched helplessly from the cliffs as his newly married daughter and her husband drowned when their boat was overtaken by a storm. He raised the chapel to her memory and kept a light burning above it to warn other sailors of the dangerous coast.

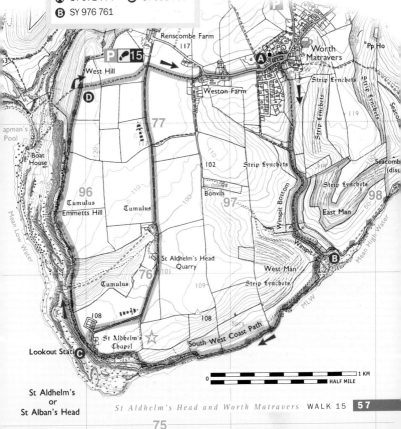

16 *Hardy Monument*

START Hardy Monument

DISTANCE 4½ miles (7.25km)

TIME 2¾ hours

PARKING Lay-by at entrance to Black Down Forest, 300 yds (274m) east of Hardy Monument

ROUTE FEATURES Mainly undulating field and woodland paths; steep climb

The rolling nature of Dorset's chalk downs offers some magnificent views, and those revealed on this walk are no exception. Starting from Black Down, the walk initially follows a long gentle valley before climbing onto a high escarpment from which, on a clear day, you can see out to the Isle of Wight. The return is through the rising woodland that surrounds the Hardy Monument.

Dorset has two famous sons by the name of Thomas Hardy; just plain Thomas, the 19th-century novelist and poet, and **Sir Thomas Masterman** the sea captain, born 71 years earlier in 1769 at Portesham. As second son, he was not destined to inherit his father's Black Down estate and so, when 12 years old, was sent to sea as a cabin boy on *HMS Helena*. He progressed through the ranks, and at the age of 24 served as lieutenant on *HMS Meleanger* under the then Captain Nelson.

The walk begins along a path signed to Corton Hill, which leaves the lane at the head of a gated forest track, opposite the lay-by to the right. Emerging from bracken, go through a gate and follow the path down an open meadow and, through a gap at the bottom, continue between an old hedge and a fence. At the end, turn through the hedge and cut right to pass through a second hedge. Keep going down the valley, heading towards a derelict farmhouse and barns.

Ⓐ Through a gate by the buildings, ignore a track to the

PUBLIC TRANSPORT None

REFRESHMENTS Seasonal ice cream and snack van by Hardy Monument, King's Arms at nearby Portesham

PUBLIC TOILETS None

ORDNANCE SURVEY MAP Explorer OL15 (Purbeck & South Dorset)

right, and instead carry on ahead along Hell Bottom at the edge of the grazing. Walk from field to field until, eventually, you reach a gate on the left that opens onto the end of a track. Follow it right to a second track and then go right again to meet a lane.

B Walk right to a junction and once more turn right, the way signed to Waddon and Portesham. 200 yds (183m) along, look for a waymark on the right by a stile in the banking above. Over that bear left to pass through an outgrown hedge and continue on a diagonal ascent of the steep escarpment, whose lower slopes were terraced by ancient farmers. At the top, go over a double stile in the wall ahead and carry on along the ridge, closing with a wall to the right,

GPS WAYPOINTS

🥾 SY 615 877		**C**	SY 624 858
A SY 623 864		**D**	SY 611 860
B SY 630 856		**E**	SY 609 869

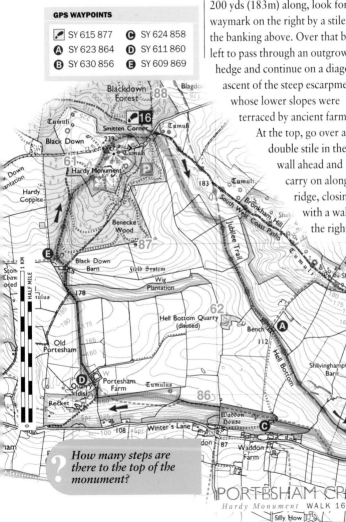

? *How many steps are there to the top of the monument?*

but watch where you put your feet, for the long grass conceals several burrows.

C Go ahead over a crossing track and bear right above a small abandoned quarry. Carry on along the ridge, passing from enclosure to enclosure and eventually emerging through a gate to join a track, which leads right to Portesham Farm.

D Over a cattle-grid, continue by the farm buildings and on, gently climbing across the fields beyond. Before long, through a gate, the track curves left and begins to sacrifice the height gained, dropping down to the ruined Black Down Barn in the base of the valley. Through a gate, bear left in front of woodland to a three-way sign some 50 yds (46m) on.

E Go right on a track rising into the wood, signed 'Hardy Monument'. Ignore side tracks and keep to the main path until you eventually reach a signed fork indicating the Hardy Monument to the right. The way continues through bracken back to the monument, which is visible ahead. Drop to the lane below the tower, where a path onto the heath opposite, signed 'Inland Route Avoiding Road', returns you to your car. ●

The Hardy Monument

Hardy entered the popular history books as captain of Nelson's flagship, *HMS Victory*, at the Battle of Trafalgar, when he kissed the brow of his mortally wounded admiral cradled in his arms as Nelson uttered his final words, 'Now I am satisfied. Thank God, I have done my duty'. Hardy's career continued, achieving First Sea Lord in 1830, and later governor of Greenwich Hospital. Hardy's final promotion was to vice admiral two years before his death in 1839, the year before the other Hardy was born. The 72-ft (22-m) tower was erected in his memory in 1844.

Fiddleford

17

START Fiddleford Manor

DISTANCE 4¾ miles (7.6km)

TIME 2¾ hours

PARKING Car park beside Fiddleford Manor

ROUTE FEATURES Undulating field and woodland paths; can be muddy when wet

Beginning on the banks of the River Stour, this walk follows the shallow valley of Darknoll Brook to the neighbouring village of Okeford Fitzpaine, where you will find some interesting curiosities. The return is via an old lane and a delightful wooded hilltop. In summer, before the fields are cropped, the going may be a little strenuous in places.

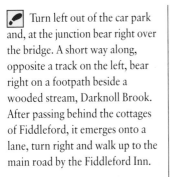 Turn left out of the car park and, at the junction bear right over the bridge. A short way along, opposite a track on the left, bear right on a footpath beside a wooded stream, Darknoll Brook. After passing behind the cottages of Fiddleford, it emerges onto a lane, turn right and walk up to the main road by the Fiddleford Inn.

? **What is the date on the side of Okeford Fitzpaine's fire pump?**

Fiddleford Manor's wooden roof

PUBLIC TRANSPORT Bus service along main road past Fiddleford

REFRESHMENTS Pubs at Fiddleford and Okeford Fitzpaine

CHILDREN'S PLAY AREA In Okeford Fitzpaine

PUBLIC TOILETS None

ORDNANCE SURVEY MAP Explorer 129 (Yeovil & Sherborne)

Attractively set above the River Stour, **Fiddleford Manor's** origins date from around 1370, when it was built by William Latimer, one-time sheriff for Somerset and Dorset. Previously much larger, it has been considerably altered, particularly during the 16th century, when it was owned by William White. You can see his initials and those of his wife, Ann, on the decoration around the doors leading from the screen passage. The building is renowned for the timber roofs above the hall and solar, formed of magnificently shaped pieces of oak jointed together in a structure that is both beautiful and functional. Look, too, at the plasterwork on the northern wall of the solar, traces of a 14th-century fresco are just visible, depicting the Annunciation.

Ⓐ Go right, but immediately over a bridge, turn left, signed 'Piddles Wood and Banbury Cross'. Walk up by the right-hand boundary, continuing through a gate into the next field. At a signpost, just beyond the crest of the hill, turn sharp left over a stile, signed Angiers Lane. Cross three paddocks via stiles, then a further stile beyond a wooden barn at Lodge Farm. Maintain your direction to cross an access bridge over a ditch in the middle of the field, before finally leaving by a small gate near the far corner of the bottom hedge.

Ⓑ Emerging onto Angers Lane, turn left, but then go right at the entrance to Angiers Farm. However, instead of following the drive, climb a stile on the right and walk up to a gate. Through that, turn left and walk across successive fields, bypassing the buildings. Beyond, keep going in the same direction across a larger meadow, a stile taking you over a lateral wire fence, part-way across. Approaching the narrowing far end of the field, look for a stile in the overgrown hedge to the right.

Ⓒ In the adjacent field, bear half left on a defined path, passing to the right of a clump of three oaks to a gate, keep heading in the same direction in the next field, dropping gently to go over a footbridge at the bottom. Keep straight ahead, crossing to a stile at the far side of the field. Now in a rough enclosure, go left and then right

Fiddleford Manor

through an opening past a garage workshop. Turn left beyond it to emerge on a street. Almost opposite to the right, a footpath leads between house gardens to the main road into the village. Go right to a junction by the Royal Oak.

D The onward route lies to the right, but first carry on to a small building by the telephone box, which houses, among other things, the village's ancient fire pump. Just

GPS WAYPOINTS

🥾 ST 801 135	**D** ST 806 110
A ST 805 131	**E** ST 802 111
B ST 804 125	**F** ST 791 127
C ST 806 119	

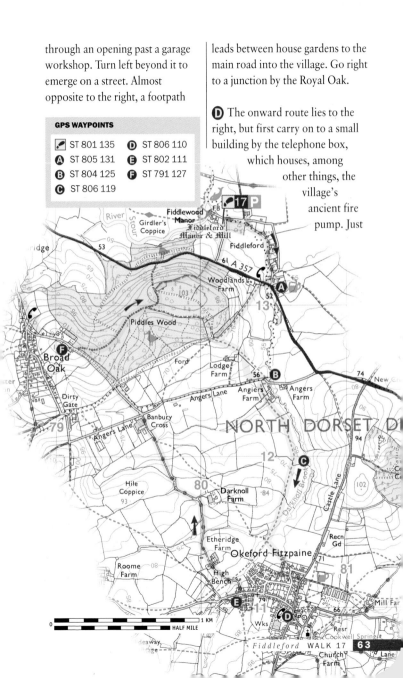

Ammonite in a cottage wall at Okeford Fitzpaine

beyond to the left is St Andrew's Church, also worthy of investigation. Return to the Royal Oak and turn left beside it. After 400 yds (365m), turn right into Darknoll Lane, signed as a halter path to Sturminster **E**.

After the last cottage, it degrades to a track, narrowing again past Darknoll Farm and finally becoming a wet, narrow green path which continues to Banbury Cross. Follow the lane directly opposite, shortly climbing beside Piddles Wood. Towards the top, turn right at the entrance to a small car park, signed Fiddleford Mill, behind which, a track leads into the trees **F**.

Within the last century, some areas of Piddles Wood have been planted with deciduous trees, but elsewhere oaks and hazel coppice reveal an older, semi-natural woodland, which you can explore along a nature trail devised by Dorset Wildlife Trust. Keep ahead past a junction, where Angiers Farm is signed off right, shortly arriving at another junction beneath a massive oak. Again ignore signs to left and right, and continue beyond, keeping to the main track signed 'Fiddleford Mill,' and ignoring paths off either side. After some 400 yds (366m), look for a path dropping left beside a mature oak and a retrospective waymark. It falls determinedly through the trees, emerging onto the A357 at the bottom. The lane back to Fiddleford Manor lies almost opposite.

Walking through Piddles Wood

It is probable that there has been a **mill** at Fiddleford since Roman times, and it appears in the Domesday survey undertaken in 1086. There is still a mill beside the river today, although it is no longer in use.

Tolpuddle and Athelhampton House

STARt Tolpuddle
DISTANCE 4¾ miles (7.6km)
TIME 2½ hours
PARKING Roadside parking in Tolpuddle
ROUTE FEATURES Woodland and field tracks; paths may be muddy after rain

This easy walk across open fields and woodland heath links two very different places, each worthy of a visit in its own right. Beginning in Tolpuddle, where the courage and determination of six men helped establish basic trade union rights, it leads to the neighbouring Athelhampton House, often considered the most beautiful country house in the county.

From beneath the Martyrs' Tree, leave Tolpuddle along Southover Lane. At a sharp bend, ¼ mile (400m) from the village, turn into a cottage drive on the right, where a bridleway is signed through a gate into a field. Cross this and the field beyond to the far corner by Southover Farm **Ⓐ**, there following a track away to the right.

? *What were the names of the Tolpuddle Martyrs?*

Backing onto the River Piddle and surrounded by delightful gardens, **Athelhampton** is one of the finest houses of its period. Begun in 1485 by Sir William Martyn, a prosperous London merchant who later became Lord Mayor, it presents a beautiful façade of warm limestone, with rows of mullioned windows, a splendid oriel and fine entrance picked out in golden Ham stone. Inside, elaborate plasterwork decorates the ceilings and sunlight streams through ancient coloured glass into rooms, furnished by the present owner's grandfather when he bought the house in 1957.

PUBLIC TRANSPORT Bus service to Tolpuddle
REFRESHMENTS Pub in Tolpuddle, tearoom at Athelhampton House
PUBLIC TOILETS None
ORDNANCE SURVEY MAP Explorer OL15 (Purbeck & South Dorset) or Explorer 117 (Cerne Abbas & Bere Regis)

Keep going past Park Farm and continue ahead at the edge of a field beyond. Pass by a gate at the far side, then a cottage to join a track and follow that to its end behind a church at Athelhampton. The entrance to Athelhampton House lies across the road to the left.

B After your visit, return to the church and follow a track away from the road past its western end. Through a couple of gates, climb into a wood and then continue generally ahead and downhill on a more open path. Emerging into a field at the far side, head down to Admiston Farm, making for a gate to the left of the buildings.

No ancient house is complete without its **ghost**, and Athelhampton has its fair share. The strangest perhaps is that of an ape, the family emblem of the Martyns and kept by them as a pet. Legend tells that after Nicholas, the last of the male line, died in 1595, the ape wandered the house in a vain search for its new master and can still be heard, scratching behind the panelling of the Great Chamber.

GPS WAYPOINTS

🖉	SY 791 944	**C**	SY 767 934
A	SY 788 940	**D**	SY 775 932
B	SY 770 941	**E**	SY 783 925

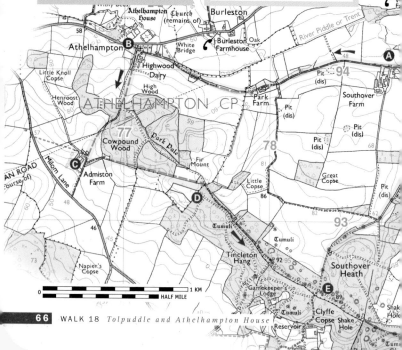

C Turn left onto a concrete track and then left again, following a rising track to a cottage at the corner of Cowpound Wood. As you approach, go into the field on the right, bypassing the cottage to enter the wood through a gate just beyond. Carry on at the edge of the trees, soon joining a track to leave through a gate on the right. Turn left along the field edge, shortly returning to woodland at the far corner.

D Keep ahead, then when you reach a fork, bear left to carry on through the trees. Ignore tracks off until, eventually, you reach a crossing at a post **E**. Now go left to wind down at the edge of Southover Heath, disregarding junctions until you finally emerge onto a drive at Southover. Turn right to reach the lane and there go left back to Tolpuddle. ●

The Tolpuddle Martyrs' statue

In 1834, in an attempt to halt a systematic reduction of their wages, **six Tolpuddle** men, under the leadership of George Loveless, a Methodist local preacher, established the Friendly Society of Agricultural Workers. Their actions angered and frightened the authorities and the men were subsequently arrested and convicted on conspiracy charges, for having sworn a secret oath. Their sentence, seven years' transportation, however, resulted in such unprecedented public outrage that they were eventually granted a free pardon. The men returned to a heroes' welcome, and their names live on as martyrs in establishing the right to free association among workers. Five of them subsequently emigrated, but James Hammett's grave can be found in the graveyard behind St John's Church. An emotive sculpture stands as a memorial to the six men outside the **Martyrs' Museum**.

19 Sturminster Newton

START Newton Mill

DISTANCE 5½ miles (8.9km)

TIME 3 hours

PARKING Car park at Newton Mill

ROUTE FEATURES Tracks, field and riverside paths; may be muddy after rain

Meandering through the lush rolling countryside of Blackmoor Vale, the River Stour once powered many mills standing beside its reed-filled banks. A few remain today, and this walk passes two of them, one still in full working order, before finishing in the attractive old town of Sturminster Newton.

From the car park, go down steps behind Newton Mill and across two bridges over the Stour to a meadow on the opposite bank. Keep ahead over the field, signed to Colber Bridge. Walk uphill and through a gate, cross a grassy bank above playing fields, and pass through another gate (with houses right) at the far side, the ongoing path still signed 'Colber Bridge'. Ignore paths off right; at the next crossing of paths turn left to reach the bridge.

This is yet another walk that conjures images from the novels of **Thomas Hardy**. Blackmoor Vale was his 'vale of little dairies', the setting for one of his greatest novels, *Tess of the D'Urbervilles*, which created quite a storm when it was first published in 1891. Hardy had previously lived for a while at Sturminster Newton, in 'Riverside Villa', a house still overlooking Colber Bridge. Remembered among his happiest years, it was during this time that Hardy wrote *The Return of the Native*.

A Cross over; the way now signed to Stalbridge Lane and Pleak House Farm, bear right on the far bank, crossing to the right-hand of two adjacent gates. Keep going by the left boundary, emerging onto Stalbridge Lane at the far side.

PUBLIC TRANSPORT Bus service to Newton

REFRESHMENTS Choice of pubs and cafés in Sturminster Newton, picnic area beside car park

PUBLIC TOILETS Adjacent to car park and in Sturminster Newton

ORDNANCE SURVEY MAP Explorer 129 (Yeovil & Sherborne)

B Turn right, signed 'Bagber', the lane degrading to a track past Oaks Farm. Carry on beyond Blackwater Bridge, the way eventually ending beside Manor Farm. Walk right onto a lane, and then right again, a short distance farther on. Soon after crossing a disued railway line, and a short distance beyond Lower Bagber Farm, go left on a path waymarked to Cutt Mill. Through successive gates, continue along a contained path. At the end, keep ahead along the edge of consecutive fields, eventually reaching a bridge across the mill weir at Cutt Mill.

Looking along the Stour to the mill

St Mary's Church at Sturminster Newton

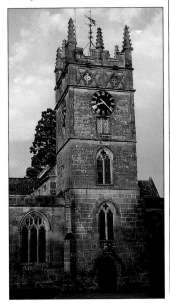

C Follow a track up to the right, passing a cottage. Just beyond, turn sharp right over a stile, dropping through Joyce's Coppice. Cross a stile at the far end and emerge into a field, where you should continue ahead above the river bank. The water is not always visible, often hiding behind a screen of reeds as you work your way downstream. After some 1¼ miles (2.1km), approaching Sturminster Newton, the path rises along a banking before continuing parallel to the water to pass beneath the still-standing portion of an old railway bridge. Where the way then divides, bear left, and go left at a crossing a little farther on, signed 'Market Place'.

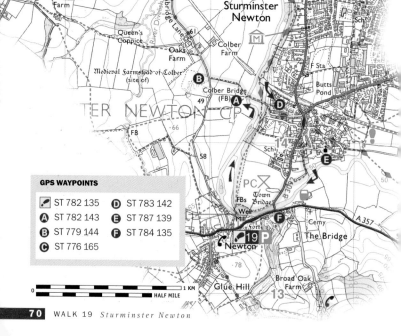

From the 10th century until the Dissolution, Sturminster Newton was held by the abbots of Glastonbury, one of whom, John Selwood, was responsible for this magnificent **church**, dedicated to St Mary. Although significantly altered in 1825, it still bears much from the original construction, perhaps the most impressive feature being the splendid wagon roof from which 14 carved angels look down upon the body of the church.

GPS WAYPOINTS

🔗 ST 782 135	Ⓓ ST 783 142
Ⓐ ST 782 143	Ⓔ ST 787 139
Ⓑ ST 779 144	Ⓕ ST 784 135
Ⓒ ST 776 165	

D Through a kissing-gate, climb to the top of the bank and follow a street out to the main road in the town. Turn right through the Market Place and bear right in front of the thatched White Hart pub, opposite which is a now dry Victorian drinking fountain and the base of the old market cross. Continue a little farther down Bridge Street before turning left into Church Lane, at the far end of which stands St Mary's Church, worth visiting for its interesting stained glass and fine wagon roof.

E Retrace your steps along Church Lane for about 150 yds (137m), looking for a path off left, signed 'Town Bridge via Coach Road'. Through a kissing-gate at the bottom, follow a tarmac path right across a paddock, returning to Bridge Street. Go left towards Town Bridge.

F After looking at the bridge, walk back towards the traffic signals and turn through a gate into the meadow on the left. Bear left upstream and, on reaching the footbridge, by the mill, cross back to the car park. ●

What is the punishment for those convicted of wilfully injuring the medieval Town Bridge?

Although not mentioned before Domesday, it is thought that there was a **mill** at Newton well before the Normans arrived. In fact, in the early 17th century, records show there were actually two mills here, one for 'grist' or grain and the other for 'fulling', the finishing process for woollen cloth. At some point, the fulling mill was pulled down and the site incorporated within the present mill, which operated commercially until 1970, producing animal feed in its latter years. For a time, its future was uncertain, then after ten years' disuse, the wheels began turning again in response to the growing interest in 'natural' foods. Ever-more stringent regulations, however, rendered the operation uneconomic, but it now operates successfully as a tourist attraction, again producing flour as it has done for centuries.

Cutt Mill

20 Harman's Cross to Corfe Castle

Railway nostalgia runs deep in many people, and so what could be better than combining a trip on a steam train with a superb walk along the Purbeck Ridge? The views from the downs are among the finest in the county and the attractions of Corfe Castle make a fitting conclusion to this splendid day out.

START Corfe Castle

DISTANCE 5½ miles (8.9km)

TIME 3¼ hours

PARKING Corfe Castle or Norden Park and Ride (charge)

ROUTE FEATURES Field paths and ridge walk; sustained climb and steep descent

You can catch the train from either Corfe Castle or Norden (where parking is sometimes easier), buying tickets to Harman's Cross, from where the walk back begins.

A Walk out of the station to the lane, cross the bridge over the line and continue up the hill beyond. Towards the top, look for a sign on the left to Wilkswood, from which an enclosed path leads beside a stonemason's yard and then around the edge of a camp site at Haycrafts Farm. Carry on across the field beyond to Quarr Farm.

B Approaching the barns, a permissive path is signed left beside them, which avoids a passage through the farmyard, which can be mucky. A track beyond leads away from the farm, winding down through the fields to an unmanned level crossing. If you have paced your walk correctly, you will see the train on which you travelled returning from Swanage. On the far side, follow the track up to the main road.

C Cross to a stile opposite and follow the field edge down to the bottom corner, signed 'Ailwood

---

PUBLIC TRANSPORT Bus and rail services to Corfe Castle and Norden

REFRESHMENTS Choice of pubs and cafés in Corfe Castle

PUBLIC TOILETS In Corfe Castle

ORDNANCE SURVEY MAP Explorer OL15 (Purbeck & South Dorset)

and Woolgarston'. Bear half right across the next field to another stile in the bottom hedge and then follow a trodden path across the next field, to find a stile towards the left in the top hedge. Now head left over the crest of a rise, walking downfield and through an opening in the bottom boundary. Then bear right, climbing to a stile and gate about three-quarters of the way along the side hedge. Cut left to a second gate, and carry on ahead over a rise to yet another gate. Cross to a final gate in the far-right corner, emerging onto a lane by Ailwood Farm.

Corfe Castle from Challow Hill

The **railway** first arrived in Swanage in 1885, a branch line from Wareham and part of the London and South Western Railway system. Its construction had faced much opposition, and it was due to the efforts of George Burt, who was behind much of Swanage's Victorian development, that the line was finally opened. Although surviving the wholesale closures of the Beeching era, its demise finally came in January 1972 and the track was taken up. But that was not the end of the story. Just three years later, the Swanage Railway Society was formed, and by 1985 trains were again running as far as Herston Halt. It took a further ten years to extend the line to Norden, with a new intermediate station at Harman's Cross being built.

D A short distance to the right, just past a cottage, turn left on a track, signed 'Ailwood Down'. Go right at the top towards Ulwell, the way undulating gently through open wood and scrub at the foot of the Purbeck Ridge. After about ½ mile (800m), look for a stone waymark to Nine Barrow Down, immediately before the second gate you come to. There, turn sharp left on a steepish track, which rises back along the slope of the escarpment. As you gain height, there is ample distraction from your effort in the view revealed to the south.

E At the top, join a grassy path and follow it west along the ridge past the several prominent bumps that are the Nine Barrows Bronze Age burial mounds. It is not long before Corfe Castle comes into view ahead, although as yet, still a good way off. To the north is the vast sweep of Pool Harbour and the Brownsea Island Nature Reserve.

F Towards the far end, go through a gate, by a transmitter mast, the main path then bears left down to Challow Farm and Corfe. However, remain on the ridge, signed to East Hill, following the vague path through a flower-rich meadow along the top of Challow Hill. At the far high-point, bear left

The ruins of **Corfe Castle** are among the most impressive in England and dramatically rise above a small strategic outcrop at a gap in the 12-mile (19.3km) Purbeck Ridge. Built towards the end of the 11th century and later strengthened by Henry I, it was regarded as one of the most impregnable fortresses in the country. Even though the engines of war had dramatically changed by the time of the Civil Wars, the castle still lived up to its reputation. It resisted a three-year siege by Oliver Cromwell before falling in 1645, not to cannon, but to treachery when a side gate was opened to let in the Parliamentary forces. In retribution, the castle defences were demolished and it was abandoned as a ruin.

GPS WAYPOINTS

🖉 SY 982 800		**D**	SY 994 811
A SY 982 800		**E**	SZ 001 813
B SY 988 796		**F**	SY 972 821
C SY 991 802		**G**	SY 961 821

74 WALK 20 *Harman's Cross to Corfe Castle*

to a stone marker indicating the top of a steep path down to Corfe. *Go carefully in wet weather, for the rock underfoot can be slippery.*

G Joining a lane at the bottom, turn right and walk up to the main street in the village. If you have parked at Norden, you can return by train, or alternatively, follow a footpath back, which leaves the main road by the National Trust car park, just to the right. ●

Corfe station

Look around Corfe Castle station. What would you not see on a modern platform?

Further Information

Walking Safety

On coastal paths, keep away from cliff edges, as they are subject to erosion and landslip, and gusts of wind can cause you to lose your balance. In summer, nettles and brambles can encroach upon paths and after rain, they will often be muddy and rocks and stiles can be slippery.

Always take with you both warm and waterproof clothing and sufficient food and drink. Wear suitable footwear, such as strong walking boots or shoes that give a good grip over stony ground, on slippery slopes and in muddy conditions. Try to obtain a local weather forecast and bear it in mind before you start. Do not be afraid to abandon your proposed route and return to your starting point in the event of a sudden and unexpected deterioration in the weather.

All the walks described in this book will be safe to do, given due care and respect, even during the winter. Indeed, a crisp, fine winter day often provides perfect walking conditions, with firm ground underfoot and a clarity of light unique to that time of the year.

The Pinnacles

The most difficult hazard likely to be encountered is mud, especially when walking along woodland and field paths, farm tracks and bridleways --the latter in particular can often get churned up by cyclists and horses. In summer, an additional difficulty may be narrow and overgrown paths, particularly along the edges of cultivated fields. Neither should constitute a major problem provided that the appropriate footwear is worn.

Global Positioning System (GPS)

What is GPS?

Global Positioning System, or GPS for short, is a fully-functional navigation system that uses a network of satellites to calculate positions, which are then transmitted to hand-held receivers. By measuring the time it takes a signal to reach the receiver, the distance from the satellite can be estimated. Repeat this with several satellites and the receiver can then triangulate its position, in effect telling the receiver exactly where you are, in any weather, day or night, anywhere on Earth.

GPS information, in the form of grid reference data, is increasingly being used in Jarrold guidebooks, and many readers find the positional accuracy GPS affords a reassurance, although its greatest benefit comes when you are walking in remote, open countryside or through forests.

GPS has become a vital global utility, indispensable for modern navigation on land, sea and air around the world, as well as an important tool for map-making and land surveying.

Follow the Country Code

- Be safe – plan ahead and follow any signs
- Leave gates and property as you find them
- Protect plants and animals, and

The train leaving Harman's Cross

take your litter home
- Keep dogs under close control
- Consider other people

(Natural England)

Useful Organisations

Campaign to Protect Rural England
128 Southwark Street,
London
SE1 0SW
Tel. 020 7981 2800
www.cpre.org.uk

English Heritage
PO Box 569, Swindon
SN2 2YP
Tel. 0870 333 1181
www.english-heritage.org.uk
South West Regional Office
Tel. 0117 975 0700

National Trust
Membership and general enquiries:
PO Box 39, Warrington,
WA5 7WD
Tel. 0870 458 4000
www.nationaltrust.org.uk

Wessex Regional Office
Tel. 01985 843600

Natural England
Northminster House,
Peterborough PE1 1UA
Tel. 0845 600 3078
www.naturalengland.org.uk

Ordnance Survey
Romsey Road, Maybush,
Southampton SO16 4GU
Tel. 08456 05 05 05 (Lo-call)
www.ordnancesurvey.co.uk

Boats on the River Frome

Ramblers' Association
2nd Floor, Camelford House,
87-90 Albert Embankment,
London SE1 7TW
www.ramblers.org.uk
Tel. 020 7339 8500

Youth Hostels Association
Trevelyan House, Dimple Road,
Matlock, Derbyshire DE4 3YH
Tel. 0870 770 8868
www.yha.org.uk

Local Organisations
Dorset Wildlife Trust
Brooklands Farm, Forston,
Dorchester DT2 7AA
Tel. 01305 264620
www.dorsetwildlife.co.uk

Dorset AONB Partnership
AONB Office, The Barracks,
Bridport Road, Dorchester,
Dorset DT1 1RN
Tel. 01305 756782
www.dorsetaonb.org.uk

Dorset County Council
County Hall, Colliton Park,
Dorchester, Dorset
DT1 1XJ
Tel. 01305 251000
www.dorsetforyou.com

**Lulworth Range and Tyneham
Range Office**
Tel. 01929 404819

Tourist Information
Southern Tourist Board
40 Chamberlayne Road, Eastleigh,
Hampshire SO5 5JH
Tel. 023 8062 5400
www.visitsoutheastengland.com

South West Tourism
Woodwater Park, Exeter,
Devon EX2 5WT
Tel. 01392 360050
www.swtourism.co.uk

*Local Tourist Information
Centres*
Blandford: 01258 454770
Bridport: 01308 424901
Dorchester: 01305 267992
Lyme Regis: 01297 442138
Poole: 01202 253253
Swanage: 01929 422885
Wareham: 01929 552740
Weymouth: 01305 785747

Public Transport
For all public transport enquiries:
Traveline: 0871 200 2233

Swanage Railway
Tel. 01929 425800
www.swanagerailway.co.uk

Ordnance Survey Maps
Explorer OL15
(Purbeck & South Dorset)
Explorer 116
(Lyme Regis & Bridport)

Explorer 117
(Cerne Abbas & Bere Regis),
Explorer 118
(Shaftesbury & Cranborne Chase)
Explorer 129
(Yeovil & Sherborne)

Answers to Questions

Walk 1: Like cattle, sheep and pigs, they have two toes, but in these woods, any such prints are more likely to be deer.

Walk 2: The points of the compass, the directions being carved on each.

Walk 3: Look in the village telephone box for the answer, just 2/6 (12.5p) per week. However, in those days, it was quite a lot of money.

Walk 4: All pines have long needles that sprout from the twig in groups of twos, threes or fives.

Walk 5: In the 17th and 18th centuries, the village was known for its beer and an inscription above the Red Lion tells you that it was one of 13 pubs.

Walk 6: It was the base plate for a chessart or cheese press, the grooves allowing the whey to escape as the cheese was formed.

Walk 7: Look at the window at the eastern end of the south aisle, where next to him is St George, the patron saint of England.

Walk 8: A cygnet.

Walk 9: Three.

Walk 10: Look at the back to find the fossil imprint of a large ammonite.

Walk 11: Have a look at the carving on the village cross.

Walk 12: *Under the Greenwood Tree* and *Far from the Madding Crowd*.

Walk 13: A Brough Superior. There is a similar one in the nearby tank museum.

Walk 14: Six, count the sides of the ancient lead font in Lady St Mary's Church.

Walk 15: Representing modern telecommunications, it commemorates radar research undertaken here during the Second World War.

Walk 16: I counted 150, but the guardian informs me that everyone seems to come down with a different number.

Walk 17: MDCCCIX, 1809, but it also carries the later date of 1895 on the front.

Walk 18: George Loveless, James Loveless, James Hammett, Thomas Standfield, John Standfield, and James Brine.

Walk 19: A plaque fixed to the parapet warns of 'transportation for life'.

Walk 20: Quite a few things, including passenger luggage trunks, a milk churn, fire buckets, and a porter's two-wheeled trolley.